Numerology

**Uncover Your Destiny with Numbers—
Details about Your Character, Life Direction,
Relationships, Finances, Motivations, and
Talents!**

SECOND EDITION

By
Jason Williams

Table of Contents

Introduction

I want to thank you and congratulate you for purchasing the book, *Numerology: Uncover Your Destiny with Numbers—Details about Your Character, Life Direction, Relationships, Finances, Motivations, and Talents.*

Over the years, Numerology has gone from just being a pagan belief to something that really captured the minds of many. As people, most of us are bound to hope that the stars have something for us, but what about numbers?

You see, our lives are made up of numbers. Our birthdates, specifically, have a lot to do with how our lives are going to be. Wouldn't it be good to know what it actually entails? Different numbers in our lives indicates different things—and it's best to learn about them so you'd get to understand yourself more!

Well, this book contains everything you need to know about how numerology affects your character, relationships, life direction, finances, and more.

Start reading this book now and learn more about yourself in no time.

Thanks again for purchasing this book, I hope you enjoy it!

CHAPTER 1

Numbers Are More than Just Numbers

When talking about Numerology, the first thing you have to keep in mind is that numbers are more than what they are. 1 isn't just 1. Your birthday isn't just your birthday for nothing. Numerologists believe that our lives are made up of numbers; that your birthday, among others, could say a lot about who you are as a person, and where your life is headed.

Maybe, you have asked yourself certain questions like, *"Why am I so unlucky?"* or *"Why does it seem like I'm attracted to people whose names start with the letter G?"* or even *"I knew that was going to happen!"* You see, these are signs that somehow, you know that the hands of fate are also playing with you, and your life, for that matter. There are patterns in your behavior, and in the way your life goes that have been dictated by the numbers in your name, the numbers in your date of birth.

Nothing Is Random

Numerology is around because of the thought that nothing in the world is "random". Everything that has happened—and will happen—in your life have already been dictated by fate, but that doesn't mean nothing could be done. Numbers actually move around on their own, too, and this is also why you still get shocked, or surprised, by what happens in your life. Thus, learning about numerology will help you be ready for what happens in your life, and to somehow get to know yourself better.

Various Patterns

As you will see in this book, numerology also involves various patterns. For one, there are individual patterns that depict a person's choices or actions, and how these actions determine what will happen in his or her life. This is why it is said that numerology could be used to determine one's true personality, understand where he's coming from, and why he is the way he is.

The second pattern is called community pattern, or how every person's numerological patterns affect the others, especially if they're all in one room together. This involves dates or other influencers, such as compatibility or passion numbers. This also denotes why some people just can't seem to do well around each other.

Lastly, there are parallel patterns, or the way some people play things off as coincidences or random doings of the universe, such as celebrities apparently dying in threes, or how natural disasters occur in connection with each other.

Understanding Numbers

By reading this book, you will finally understand how numbers influence your life—and what you can make out of them, starting with the birth path number in the following chapter.

CHAPTER 2

Birth Path/Destiny Number—What Numbers Say about Your Character

First up is your Birth Path Number. Basically, this is the date of your birth (without the year), cut in half and added to get the right result. Birth Path Numbers are known as the foundation of numerology, and that's why it's important for you to understand what they could bring.

For example, suppose your birthday is on the 18th. It would go like this:

18 = 1 + 8 = 9. Your Birth Path Number is 9.

If your birthday is 23, it would be: 23 = 2 + 3 = 5. Your birth number is 5, and so on.

1 (SUN)
Those born on 1st, 10th, 19th or 28th

Communicate with your senior colleagues; they will help you with assignments. Reorganise your daily schedule to make sure you have time for loved ones. Avoid bingeing at all cost!
Lucky Days: Sun, Mon

2 (MOON)
Those born on 2nd, 11th, 20th or 29th

Keep yourself updated with the latest developments at work to avoid any miscommunication. Money matters might trouble you. Students may go abroad for higher studies.
Lucky Days: Sun, Mon

3 (JUPITER)
Those born on 3rd, 12th, 21st or 30th

Avoid signing any partnership deal this week. You could suffer from a severe financial crunch. Eat at home as far as possible to avoid stomach infection. Respect the feelings of elders.
Lucky Days: Fri, Tue

4 (URANUS)
Those born on 4th, 13th, 22nd or 31st

You may face some disappointment at both the personal and professional front. Fret not; you will soon be back with a bang! Take care of your finances. A letter will bring happy tidings.
Lucky Days: Sun, Mon

5 (MERCURY)
Those born on the 5th, 14th or 23rd

On the personal front, those in a relationship must be extra cautious about the feelings of their partners. At work, you could be involved in an argument. Try to control your temper.
Lucky Days: Tue, Thur

6 (VENUS)
Those born on the 6th, 15th or 24th

An optimistic attitude, coupled with enthusiasm, will help you win the confidence of your superiors. Matters will be harmonious on the domestic front. A long-lost friend will contact you.
Lucky Days: Fri, Tue

7 (NEPTUNE)
Those born on the 7th, 16th or 25th

Avoid a confrontation with your colleagues. Be practical as far as possible and everyone will understand your point of view. Plan a holiday with your family. Get a health check-up done.
Lucky Days: Sun, Mon

8 (SATURN)
Those born on the 8th, 17th or 26th

A pleasant period to start a brand new project. Don't let trivial arguments come in the way of advancements in your career. Weekend travel is on the cards. Make sure your house is secure!
Lucky Days: Fri, Tue

9 (MARS)
Those born on the 9th, 18th or 27th

Chances of having conflicts on the work front seem a little high. Avoid arguing with seniors. Be prepared to explain your stand. Muscle pains could force you to take leave for a few days.
Lucky Days: Fri, Tue

https://www.pinterest.com/pin/346425396316900889/

Above is a simple astrology chart that shows the Birth Path Number. It shows how different one person can be from the other.

Birth Path Number Meanings

Below, you'd learn more about the said birth path numbers!

Number 1: The Primal Force (born on the 1st, 10th, 19th, 28th)

First, of course, is number 1, also known as the Primal Force. As it is first of all numbers, it is also the symbol of the sun, one dominating factor in the universe.

People whose birth number is 1 are often born leaders, and are quite imaginative and creative by nature. They could easily persuade people, but prefer to work alone, even without managers or subordinates.

Number 1s are quite determined and ambitious. They are strong-willed, but could also be stubborn. They do not rest until their demands are satisfied, but if they don't get what they want, they tend to throw tantrums and just can't seem to understand that life would not always work their way.

When they have kids, they are quite gentle, and are also quite sensitive to others' needs. It's often easy for them to achieve their dreams, especially if they are supported by the ones they love.

Number 2: The All Knowing (born on the 2nd, 11th, 20th, 29th)

Often deemed as the opposite of Primal Forces, number 2s are romantic and gentle, while still being able to be creative and smart, artistic, and imaginative. Most of their strength is in their mind, or their mental abilities.

All Knowings are also dreamers. They kind of live in their minds and their so-called spiritual clouds. This makes it easy for them not to be too materialistic.

Oftentimes, they are also soft and forgiving. They don't like holding grudges, and as much as they could, they prevent themselves from being aggressive because they believe that having enough self-control would help them succeed in life.

However, they like avoiding heavy labor because they know they could be emotionally and physically vulnerable.

In relationships, they want to have spiritual connections with their partners, and their sexual satisfaction isn't too important, and only comes second to them. They do not like being with people who are emotionally or spiritually weak. They'd rather dream than be around people who do not have dreams themselves, but know they also have to work hard to make those dreams come true, helping them achieve success. They believe that nothing is impossible!

Number 3: The Creative Child (born on the 3rd, 12th, 21st, 30th)

Number 3s are often busy, strong-willed, and ambitious. They're often energetic, and know they can't be lethargic because when that happens, they won't be able to make their dreams come to life.

They also like working alone, and believe that groupmates or subordinates would just make the work harder. They don't like relying on other people, and they do not trust others easily. When working with others, they expect obedience and respect. Otherwise, they'd rather work alone. They are brilliant leaders.

It's also easy for Number 3s to make plans and make them come true. They also have great endurance and do not get easily tired, and are often considered to be powerful and strong. They also have little time for love or romance because they don't believe that relationships are as great as "the chase".

Number 4: The Salt of the Earth (born on the 4th, 13th, 22nd, 31st)

The famed mathematician Pythagoras once said that the number 4 is a symbol of support and foundation. This is why Number 4s often have the aura of significance and importance. They are quite patient, communicative, and reliable. They could not be shaken, especially when it comes to their principles as they believe them all the way to the end.

The problem with 4s, though, is the fact that while they are patient, when they don't get to express themselves for a time, they just blow up big-time. When this happens, it's hard to restrain them. They have to let their steam out.

They are physically strong, but their intellects do not suffer, too. This is also why they are easily pressured, especially when they feel like they couldn't give what others are expecting of them.

Number 4s are also intuitive and honest. Basically, their motto in life is *what you see is what you get.* They also hate wasting time on frivolous, superficial people, and value honesty and loyalty more than anything else.

Number 5: The Dynamic Force (born on the 5th, 14th, 23rd)

Symbolized by the Pentagram, Number 5s often aim for perfection in more than one aspect of life—just as the pentagram points towards a couple of directions. While the Pentagram is considered by many as good omen, those with this birth number are often swayed into the unknown, and may encounter a lot of confusion in life.

Although it's also good that they have many interests in life, sometimes, it leads them to a place of darkness and may make them feel like they have to continually search for something in life.

However, what's great about 5s is that they are extremely friendly, and have no problem relating to others. They're also interesting individuals so people are drawn to them.

The problem, though, is that oftentimes, they could also be sarcastic, which does not sit well with others. They are also curious, which leads them to gossip or always feel like they have to know what's hot and what's not first, which makes them gain unnecessary information that could also be overwhelming.

Number 5s love to take risks. They are not scared of bold and big ideas, and it's also easy for them to adapt to any situation—as long as they don't let the dark thoughts take over.

Number 6: The Caretaker (born on the 6th, 15th, 24th)

The 6s are some of the most charming and harmonious people around. They are beautiful, healthy, full of love, and filled with wisdom.

They also desire for perfection and for the admiration or love of many, but it's not really a problem for them because they are naturally magnetic, and people are easily drawn towards them. Even if they don't look perfect in the eyes of others, they still have the X-Factor, and that's why a lot of opportunities open up for them. They are often said to have "special grace".

Number 6s are easily trusted, but while they have so much love to give, love always doesn't come easy for them. It's hard for them to find people they could consider their one true loves, but the great thing is that it's not hard for them to achieve their other goals in life.

Only problem though is that by being naturally maternal and caring, some people tend to take advantage of them, and of course, that could really hurt.

Number 7: The Seeker (born on the 7th, 16th, 25th)

7s are often incomprehensible and mysterious. They are often called unsolved mysteries or dark horses, which makes them intriguing to some, and to others, just people who could be considered wallflowers.

Seekers are also often calm and quiet and have a natural inclination to being alone, and to working on their own. They are harmonious introverts, but never really feel rejected or only because being alone is mostly their choice.

The problem is that sometimes, they could be quite cold and volatile, and when this happens, they find it hard to control themselves. But, when they're at their best, they are warm, non-judgmental, and are also attentive. They could also be sociable at times, especially when they like the people around them.

However, when they're away from people they trust or consider family, they feel alone, and they feel like they couldn't relate to the world, making it hard for them to adjust at school or work, or any new event in their lives.

Number 8: Balance and Power (Born on the 8th, 17th, 26th)

Number 8s are often associated with money and business skills. However, their true potential isn't just all about money or wealth, but something way deeper. Number 8s are quite artistic—the only problem is that they sometimes find it hard to tap into their inner artistry, and aren't confident enough to push through with what they want.

However, 8s could change their lives because they are naturally ambitious and energetic, and are capable of doing amazing things in their lives. They are also hard workers who choose to work with their intellects and emotions, because they know that when those two work together, they'll be able to get more viable results, and a better quality of work.

While misunderstood, those under this birth number could actually have deep connections with others, and are capable of doing great sacrifices, which also makes them vulnerable to being used when they're with the wrong people. They always look for harmonious relationships in life, and want to maintain spiritual fellowship with the people in their lives.

Number 9: Global Awareness (Born on the 9th, 18th, 27th)

9s are complicated individuals, but are naturally sensitive, aristocratic, and harmonious. Their intuition is great, but they often forget to listen to it. They are broad thinkers, wide readers, and are also well-educated—that's why they often assume positions of leadership, whether in their careers or in relationships.

Sometimes, they tend to make conclusions out of what already happened, and what could happen because of their sensitivity and perception. It's also easy for them to tolerate others' shortcomings, but when they reach the ends of their ropes, they tend to cut off people in their lives easily. They hate having toxic people in their lives, and tend to keep just a small circle of friends, but a couple of acquaintances.

Highly philosophical, they often aim for perfection, and put the highest demands on themselves. Often, they also expect the best from other people because they know they can give them their best, and are disappointed when others are not up par with their expectations. They love doing good things for others, and are often charitable, and have great artistic tastes. They could also be artistic, creative, and musically talented.

They're sexy and charming, but could also be introverted and inferior to others. Sometimes, they also find it hard to express themselves, are quite deep, but cannot easily trust people, even those already in their life, because they are scared to lose dignity and trust the wrong people.

They learn from their own mistakes, making them achieve success, even after a long climb to the top.

CHAPTER 3

Life Path Number—What It Says About Your Life Direction

Next is your Life Path Number, which could say a lot about the direction your life may take.

The Life Path Number is the result of adding single digits in your full date of birth. Take a look at the image below to understand it better:

EXAMPLE 1: JANUARY 5, 1976

JANUARY = 1 (1st Month)	=	**1**
5 = 0 + 5	=	**5**
1976 = 1 + 9 + 7 + 6	=	**23**
	Add =	**29**
	29 = 2 + 9 =	**11**

http://www.tokenrock.com/stock/num_lpcharts1.gif

As you can see in the image above, the person's birthday is January 5, 1976. This could then be cut into:

January = 1 (First month of the year) = 1

5 = 5

1976 = 1 + 9 + 7 + 6

Add them all up:

$1 + 5 + 2 + 9 = 29$

$29 = 2 + 9 = \mathbf{11}$

This means that the person's Life Path Number is 11.

Let's try another example to make it clearer.

EXAMPLE 2: NOVEMBER 21, 1947		
NOVEMBER = 11 (11th Month)		= 11
21 = 2 + 1		= 3
1947 = 1 + 9 + 4 + 7		= 21
	Add	= 35
	35 = 3 + 5 =	**8**

http://www.tokenrock.com/stock/num_lpcharts2.gif

In the example above, the person's date of birth is November 21, 1947.

November = 11 (11th month of the year) = 11

$21 = 2 + 1 = 3$

$1947 = 1 + 9 + 4 + 7 = 21$

Add them all up:

$11 + 3 + 21 = 35 = 3 + 5 = \mathbf{8}$. This time, 8 is the Life Path Number.

Numerology Life Paths-at-a-glance	
For quick reference, the Numerology themes look like the following:	
Life Path 1	The Leader
Life Path 2	The Inward Creator/Motivator
Life Path 3	The Informed Speaker/Communicator
Life Path 4	The Realist, Problem Solver, Builder of Order
Life Path 5	The Unending Talent
Life Path 6	The Responsible One/The Server
Life Path 7	The Source of Knowledge. Expert/Thinker/Analyze
Life Path 8	The Material Manifester
Life Path 9	The Humanitarian
Life Path 11	The In-the-Moment Intuitive
Life Path 22	The Material and Humanity Master
Life Path 33	The Spiritual Teacher

http://michellepayton.com/wp-content/uploads/2013/07/BMP-LIfePathSum.gif

As you can see in the chart above, certain descriptions are given for different life path numbers. 11s are in the moment, and 8s are material manifesters. This way, you somehow easily get to see what a person is like, and how his life might be like.

Read on for more detailed descriptions!

Life Path Number Descriptions

1: Leadership

It is but accurate that 1 is really related to leadership, to being a champion, or being above everyone else. Those with 1 as their life

15

path number often have bright personalities and positive nature that makes it easy for them to go through life without having a hard time.

When they desire things, they desire intently and make use of their strong spirit, creativity, and originality to run businesses, or to be amazing at work or at home.

If 1 is your life path number, it is recommended that you start projects from scratch and if you make mistakes, just learn from them. Getting others' opinions might just make you sway off course and that's not what you'd want to happen. It's best that you learn to make your own decisions, and you don't let the advice of others make you feel incompetent.

Be practical and prudent, and you'd surely achieve what you want. Patience should also be one of your core virtues, and make sure that you surround yourself with people who believe in your cause, and who you know would listen to you and follow you—without forcing you to change decisions, especially when you know you're in the right.

And, make sure to take risks, be brave, and take full responsibility of your action; only then will you receive true success in life.

2: Collaboration, Peacemaking

A sense of unity is important for those whose life path number is 2. They are the best assistants and spouses, and always make sure that they work in accordance to what their leader wants, and that there should be harmony around them, whether at home or at work.

It's easy for 2s to learn from others' mistakes and apply the lessons they have learned in their own lives. They cannot tolerate disagreements and times when life doesn't seem to be harmonious, or when life is imbalanced. They do their best to save the world, literally and figuratively.

If this is your life path number, remember that it's best for you to stay thoughtful and friendly, because these would not go unnoticed. It's important that you leave good impressions on the people you meet. Always act calmly and rationally, even during times when you feel pressured or when you feel like you might crack. Remember that the success of your life relies on your ability to smoothen out the rough edges.

Also, remember that it's okay to ask for help when you feel like you cannot understand what's going on anymore. You are indispensable, yes, but some others around you are, too. If you understand that others around you are significant on earth, too, you'll easily be able to achieve what you want and find peace in your life.

3: Creativity

Those whose life path is the number 3 believe that the essence of their lives lies in self-expression. It's easy for them to entertain others and be sociable, and often have friends they could trust. Because of this, some people envy them, but those who see their potential know how intelligent they are.

It's easy for those with this life path number to acquire knowledge from whatever surrounds them, and if this is your number, you have to make sure that you use your acquired knowledge wisely. Try to focus on one thing first before moving on to the other to complete this certain box of knowledge. However, it's also naturally easy for you to lose interest in one thing and move on to the other, but if you can, try to avoid this from happening.

You are naturally gifted—you just have to know how to express yourself, or else what you have learned might go to waste. You're actually enthusiastic and magnetic enough that you can easily influence the people around you.

Try to understand that not everything might go your way, and there is nothing wrong with that. You should learn to balance idealism and realism to make use of your creativity and not become too disappointed in life.

It would also be good if you could choose your expressions better and if you would not be overly critical of things. Time your jokes, and you'd find more people interested in you.

4: Trustworthiness, Practicality

Equality is prevalent for those whose life path number is 4. In short, you have to make use of a logical, strongly-aligned foundation so that the decisions you'll make would have amazing, long-term effects in your life.

The thing with being a number 4 is that you should pay attention to what you already have in your life to achieve the kind of success you want. It's about learning to be content instead of dreaming too big and too unrealistic that you forget to appreciate what you have.

It's also important that you demonstrate virtuosity and practicality in your life. Choose things and careers that you know are close to you, and you know you can do well.

Try to evaluate the projects you're currently doing to figure out how you can do your best, and how you can make life the best there is. Focus on implementing your plans, try to be conservative, and always be responsible for your own actions. And, please try not to shy away from responsibilities, especially if you know you can do them, no matter how small they are.

Prevent yourself from jealousy, acrimony, or envy.

5: Adventures, Freedom

5s are naturally free spirits. It's important for them to fight for this freedom, and not let anyone else take it away from them. Being naturally intelligent, and knowing how to accept and understand various kinds of religions and beliefs, it's easy for them to set a quest for freedom.

This also gives them a chameleon's mind, which makes it easy for them to adjust to any given situation. They are interested in life, and whatever it entails, and believe they are the storytellers of their own lives.

If this is your life path number, you should realize that you don't have to try too hard. You're already magnetic and charming, and as they say, *if it ain't broke, don't fix it.*

However, when you're around new people, try not to be so sardonic because they might not take nicely to it. Just always stick to your goals, and know what you're bound to do. While being a hippie kind of person, you should still be responsible.

It's natural for you to be messy especially when you let your imagination run wild, but know that it's best if you don't let this messiness close your mind. Try to balance everything out.

6: Humanism, Family

For those whose life path number is 6, they are fulfilled when they see themselves adapting to situations, being in close contact with others, and trying to put themselves in others' shoes. They know that in life, they're bound to have many responsibilities and that they should adapt to various situations, but they really have no problems doing so.

They often dream of having families, or even family-like settings and believe this could give them satisfaction and happiness, and are bound to play peacemakers especially when they know people need their extra help. Even disagreements do not make their minds foggy. They know these are needed to help them grow.

If this is your number, it's important for you to tap into your own selflessness. This is one of your core values, so it's important that you make use of this in your life. Try to be sympathetic and understanding, and always express your admiration for art and beauty when you feel like it.

7: Knowledge, Exploration

Those under number 7 are deep thinkers and often look into everything. They believe that research is important in life, and they believe in standing for their own beliefs and are prepared to argue because of these.

It's also easy for them to be conscious, especially when they know people are suffering around them. They also easily relate to people who can understand their habits and their way of thinking.

If this is your number, you might find fulfillment in being a philosopher or historian. Surround yourself with beautiful things, and with people who are "full of life". Collect art if you can so you could stay inspired.

8: Power, Wealth

If 8 is your life path number, you can be assured that fate is already promising you power and prosperity. The only thing you have to do is make sure you do not become dependent on anyone around you, and that you should work on your own, from the ground, to get the power and wealth that would make you complete.

It would also be good if you could choose activities that require great responsibility and focus because these are the ones that would make you feel right, and make you feel that you're doing something important.

Keep empathizing, and always nurture your perception. Never lose hope and courage and you'd be fulfilled all the days of your life.

9: Compassion, Philanthropy

Compassion rules over those with life path number of 9 because they are naturally sensitive, and could easily appreciate sounds, art, music, nature, and even the various personalities around them. These awaken your mind, and improve your insight.

If this is your number, you're probably also interested in mysticism and you have this irrational need to learn more not just about yourself, and also from whatever's going on around you. You might also have the gift of extra-sensory perception (ESP).

Your greatest dream may be this incessant need to roam, to be more developed as a person, and to give love and sympathy to those who need it. It isn't hard for you to give to others, even with what little you have. You'd find it great when you are rewarded for your kindness, because it happens when you least expect it.

Remember that you'll naturally attract attention—use it for the best.

11: Spiritual Messenger

Being under this life path could be quite challenging. This is because it's a combination of birth numbers 1 and 2, which as you might know by now work on opposite ways.

This means that you might be naturally ambitious, but could often be easily confused because you're independent and energetic, even when making decisions. While these may make you strong, no one can deny the fact that you might also be delicate and sensitive—especially when it comes to your work.

Thus, it is important for you to be strong and realize that even if certain challenges come your way, it doesn't mean that you should just give up your dreams and forget about what really matters to you.

Do not just dream—do more than that.

22: Master Builder

By being under this life path, you are already under two important powers in life. It is upon you to transform the archetype of your personality from your mind into the real world.

You should learn to see challenges are just challenges and not roadblocks to get on the path to success. It's also important that you make a list of your goals to understand what you truly want. Don't just go through life like a leaf in the wind.

When you get to know yourself, you also get to build great things for the world around you. This means it might even be good for you to be with the government or big organizations!

33: Master Teacher

Lastly, if your life path number is 33, it means that you'll be able to tap into a harmony of powers and balance, and that it's important to use both creativity and logic so you could persevere well.

It's also natural for you to bestow generosity, but make sure that you leave some for your own, and you don't allow yourself to become a doormat. You can overcome your emotions, so do not allow them to control you.

You are a master of love and joyous energy. Let positivity rule your life, and you'd find the success you've always dreamed of!

CHAPTER 4

Compatibility Number—Compatibility and Relationships

Next, it's time to learn what numbers say about compatibility and relationships. This involves both life path and birth/destiny numbers. Take a look at this chart below:

Your Energy Number (Birth Date Number)	Best Choice Cities having Energy Number	Second Option Cities having Energy Number	Avoid Choosing Cities having Energy Number	Neutral effect Cities having Energy Number
1	1	4, 8, 9	6, 7	2, 3, 5
2	2	7, 8, 9	5	1, 3, 4, 6
3	3	5, 6, 7, 9	4, 8	1, 2
4	4	1, 6	3, 5	2, 7, 8, 9
5	5	1, 3, 6, 7, 8, 9	2, 4	---
6	6	3, 4, 9	1, 8	2, 5, 7
7	7	2, 3	1, 9	4, 5, 6, 8
8	8	1, 2, 4	3, 6	5, 7, 9
9	9	1, 2, 3, 6	7	4, 5, 8

http://1.bp.blogspot.com/_BA3g3-WuKQw/THzqGwYf1pI/AAAAAAAAAF4/DOjqNhy_mt4/s1600/comparison.png

You see, the chart above shows which numbers are compatible, and which should be avoided. This one below, meanwhile, shows traits of the numbers so you could easily compare.

YOU \ PARTNER	1	2	3	4	5	6	7	8	9
1	get ready for sparks & high spirits!	encourage your quieter partner to share your busy social life	you work well together & enjoy life to the fullest	dedication & practicality in your partner will be heightened	together you will want to pursue fun & excitement	encourage your partner to keep their life challeging	your strengths encourage your partner to be more sociable	share your secrets and achievements together	your open manner encourages your partner to be more vocal
2	encourage your partner to be in touch with their emotions	sympathize over heartbreak & enjoy creative activities together	bring out the gentle creativity in your partner	you are a good listener for your more cautious partner	you will lift your partner's spirits when they are down	endeavor to enjoy the beautiful things in life together	you are an ideal confidant & you both appreciate beauty	remember the importance of being in touch with emotions	you inspire your partner & encourage them to be more open
3	enjoy the effort you put into things you do together	give your gentle partner reassurance and confidence	you will be ideal sounding boards & confidants for each other	encourage your partner to pursue their ambitions & dreams	give your partner the variety & stimulation they need	encourage the pursuit of beauty in your partner	charm your partner into being more expressive & open	encourage your partner to be realistic in their goals	help your partner be more determined & confident
4	encourage your independent partner to be a team player	you bring out the practical side in your partner	inspire your partner to work hard for their dreams	you enjoy being open & practical together	Remind your partner that the little things matter too	encourage your partner to express their artistic nature	encourage your partner to keep a balanced perspective	you will help your partner strive for their goals	you bring out the practical achiever in each other
5	encourage a less cautious & direct approach to life	you bring out the more lively side of your partner	you are well matched & will have a lot of fun together	try to bring out the sensation-seeker in your partner	take advantage of your adventurous natures	encourage your partner to seek variety in their life	motivate your partner to be successful in work & love	together you will be able to achieve success	encourage self-expression & confidence in your partner
6	help your partner take it easy & appreciate beauty in life	try to learn to enjoy appreciating beauty together	remind your partner to appreciate a slower pace	share your love of home & home-making with one another	you will encourage your partner's artistic side	enjoy beauty, happiness & serenity together	enjoy and share your ideas & hobbies together	bring out the spiritual side in your partner	you will be a confidant & encourage firm boundaries
7	you will encourage your partner to share their feelings	you bring out the romantic side of one another	encourage your partner to be ambitous & confident	help to highlight your partner's aesthetic & artistic side	you will help bring peach & calm into your partner's life	start to enjoy creativity & the beauty of nature together	together your idealists will put the world to rights	encourage more spiritual pursuits in one another	try to bring out the sensitive side in one another
8	use your confidence to stimulate your partner	encourage your partner to be more productive	encourage each other to make the most of every day	you will bring out the high achiever in your partner	your fun-loving & adventurous natures will bring many laughs	bring out the desire to enjoy the good things	you will charm your partner into being more social	you ignite each other's success	encourage your partner to express their true feelings
9	help your partner stay centered when they are stressed	you will help your friend stay creative & driven	help your partner focus their energy in the right direction	encourage the practical side of each other each day	stimulate your partner to keep them out of a rut	you are able to confide & express feelings to each other	enhoy calm quiet discussions together	push each other & work on your weak points	you will be at ease & relaxed together

http://bit.ly/1CTlpgA

http://numerologylove.weebly.com/
uploads/1/0/2/1/10212962/9728489_orig.png

The above chart shows various traits of the different numbers and how they could work together.

You can understand this better with these comparisons below:

1 and 1: Two leaders may find it hard to compromise because they both want to lead, and they both want to be independent. In time, they might even begin to compete, which might not be good for the relationship.

1 and 2: These work together as long as they know their roles in the relationship. 1 could be the breadwinner, and 2 could take care of the house.

1 and 3: These could work together as they're both lively and compassionate. They could acknowledge each other's accomplishments without hurting their egos.

1 and 4: It may be hard for these two to go together because 1 may not like 4's desire for control, and 4 might often be frustrated with 1's ways.

1 and 5: These numbers are quite compatible, and they appreciate having freedom in the relationship. They would not smother each other, which makes them an ideal couple.

1 and 6: These represent a power struggle that's just waiting to happen, and could be unhealthy, because they also want to be independent.

1 and 7: While they are on opposite sides of the spectrum, they actually work well together. 1 is the motivator, while 7 provides amazing insights, making it quite an inspiring relationship.

1 and 8: This may work for a business standpoint, but not as a relationship. Both are just demanding and assertive and that wouldn't do well for romance. They both hate negative feedback.

1 and 9: 9 could be quite selfless, which makes it easy for the relationship to work. He could give way to 1, and 1 will be able to work on understanding his partner, too.

2 and 2: This is a perfect match of souls who have love in their cores, which means the relationship would easily work.

2 and 3: These have good chemistry, and are also both full of humor so you can expect that the relationship would be light and easy, making it good for those involved.

2 and 4: Comfort is easy in this relationship, as this is considered a stable pairing. 2 would take care of the home, and 4 would gladly provide.

2 and 5: Because 5 needs freedom and 2 needs family stability, it's important for these two to have an insane amount of chemistry for their relationship to work.

2 and 6: This one is another perfect combination as they are both caring and family-oriented.

2 and 7: These numbers may not work quite well because they both have different needs that might not be addressed in the relationship.

2 and 8: These numbers work well because both of them know exactly what they're doing and what they want in the relationship, so there is no power struggle between them.

2 and 9: It could go either way for these numbers. 9 is naturally caring, but 2 needs a lot of attention, and one could be pissed off about the other. A lot of work and chemistry has to be around for this to work.

3 and 3: Both these numbers have so much social and creative potential, which makes the relationship always interesting and adventurous. However, they also need to show control so they would not explode.

3 and 4: It could also go either way, but more often than not, this does not work because they both just couldn't give at the same time. It would be like a power struggle all the time.

3 and 5: Both these numbers are sociable, which might make it easy for them to understand each other. They also would take on various opportunities together!

3 and 6: 6 provides stability while 3 is full of enthusiasm so this pairing could work, and could lead to a happy, stable relationship.

3 and 7: This could be quite polarizing as 3 and 7 are literally on different ends of the spectrum. 7 is quite a homebody, while 3 would always seek adventure, and it would be tiring for them to control each other.

3 and 8: Extra effort is needed in this relationship again, because of 3's incessant need to travel and move around—it could be tiring, too.

3 and 9: This, meanwhile, could be quite a perfect combination because both these numbers are determined to be creative in a variety of ways. They are both sociable and creative, and could have unending joy together.

4 and 4: This could be quite a secure relationship, and might be good for long-lasting relationships as they both believe in stability. The relationship would also be full of love, romance, and growth.

4 and 5: Both of these are temperamental so the relationship could really be challenging. They also have different ways of communicating and it might not work with the others' ways. Respect is needed for this one to work.

4 and 6: This is quite a traditional pair that could really make for a comforting, stable relationship. 6 always takes the lead, while 4 could take care of the home. Security is needed in for this to work best.

4 and 7: This could be quite a serious relationship, where security is the top priority. It may not be as playful or passionate as others, but is rock solid and could withstand any challenge.

4 and 8: Both of these numbers work hard and understand the need to get ahead in this life. This is also why the relationship could be comforting.

4 and 9: These two couldn't be more different from the other and it's rare for this kind of pairing to work. They are mostly focused on what they could do for the world, and not for their relationship.

5 and 5: Two 5s make one great whole. They are quite compatible with each other, and are both open to ideas that could spice up the relationship. They also easily know what the other is thinking!

5 and 6: A lot of compromise is needed for this relationship to work because 6 is quite controlling, and 5 is a free spirit. 5 may just want to play the field, while 6 always want a strong, steady relationship—and that's why relationships with these numbers may not really work together.

5 and 7: This is a relationship that could be free of rules. They could work well together, but other times, they might also be tired of the need for freedom, and would want a strong, committed relationship.

5 and 8: Both of these numbers don't always follow the rules, which might also make or break the relationship as there may come a time when they could both be rebellious, especially when it comes to finances.

5 and 9: This relationship may not work well because both are inclined to having busy schedules. They are also both on a constant need for transition, which means that a stable relationship may just be off the hook.

6 and 6: Though they are both romantic, they are also practical, which puts balance in the relationship. They are realists, so they'd do their best to make the relationship work, and it's not just all about dreams.

6 and 7: They have different ideas about what a relationship is and should be like, so the relationship might not really work the way they want it to. Sexual attraction is prevalent, but might not be able to save the relationship.

6 and 8: Both of these numbers are open and positive and bring both their ideas to the table so they'd have a relationship that works, and so both of them would be happy.

6 and 9: This is quite a respectful, compatible relationship. 9 allows 6 to be recognized, and 6 also allows 9 to be himself—this is essential especially when they already have a family. However, they both need to keep an eye on the budget!

7 and 7: The good thing about this is that they'd both understand each other's eccentricities, which makes this a really compatible, stable pairing. They work on the same wavelength, which means they'd look in one direction and steer the relationship to the right path.

7 and 8: Even though sexual attraction is high and they physically work well together, emotionally, they just don't quite fit the right way. 7 is a private person, and 8 wants to dominate but 7 won't let him. It would be such a tiring power struggle so it's not advisable for them to be together.

7 and 9: They're both passionate so they'd never be neutral when it comes to expressing themselves, and this could work either positively or negatively. However, they are both deep and spiritual, and this could really save the relationship especially when used the right way.

8 and 8: With loads of romance and passion, this is considered the dynamic duo. This relationship might work and might stay stable for a long time. The problem lies with the couple not being able to express themselves well, so it's important that they learn to respect each other and not be afraid to say what they want.

8 and 9: This is one of the most challenging couplings of all. They are both motivated, but in different ways, and that's why clashes are inevitable. 8 wants to prove himself as a leader, while 9 has that ideological, creative mind. This is why they both have respect and appreciation for each other so that the relationship could work. When it does, it becomes of the most beautiful relationships of all.

9 and 9: This is quite a promising relationship and is also refreshing and intellectually stimulating. They are both selfless, so they'd do their best to make the relationship work, and do what they can to make each other happy. They'd use the relationship to learn from each other, too.

CHAPTER 5

Money Number—What Numbers Say about Finances

Of course, the numbers also have something to say about your finances. You could use the life path number for this, or you can also use the date of your birth, minus the year, together with the current year. You can check the image below for example:

Add up the individual digits for your

MONTH of Birth + DAY of Birth + CURRENT YEAR (2011)

Example: Birth Date September 23:

$9 + 2 + 3 + 2 + 0 + 1 + 1 = 18$

If the result is a double digit, reduce it until you have a single digit:

$1 + 8 = 9$

RESULT: This is a **9** year for the person born on September 23 in *any* year.

http://www.astrologykarmaandyou.com/images/chart1.jpg

As you can see in the image above, one's birthday is September 23. This means:

September = 9 (9th month of the year) = 9

$23 = 2 + 3 = 5$

2011 (let's pretend that this is the current year) = 2 + 0

$+ 1 + 1 = 4$

$$9 + 5 + 4 = 18$$

$$18 = 1 + 8 = 9$$

This now means that the person's money number is 9.

Let's have another example. Let's say your birthday is October 18. Now, the current year is 2015. It would then be:

October = 10 (1oth month of the year) = $1 + 0 = 1$

$$18 = 1 + 8 = 9$$

$$2015 \text{ (current year)} = 2 + 0 + 1 + 5 = 8$$

This means:

$1 + 9 + 8 = 18$

$18 = 1 + 8 = 9$

Again, 9 is the Money Number. This is also why it's said that you can actually use your life path number for this!

Money Numbers

Read on and learn more about what your money number says about you:

Money Number 1

If 1 is your money number, you're mostly destined to have financial freedom in your life. 1 has the energy of new beginnings, so if you have financial troubles, you can expect that you'll easily move on from them.

Being an excellent leader, you have lots of opportunities for financial gain and growth. Just make sure that you take opportunities that allows you to lead as much as you can instead of being a mere follower because your finances might dwindle that way.

Money Number 2

2 could have a lot of challenges when it comes to financial stability. It does not have the vibration of wealth, and just couldn't stop giving to others. Monetary system is mostly flawed for number 2s.

There are also a lot of delays that number 2 might face when it comes to gaining money. Make sure that you strive hard and get on a career related to business or finance to attract money. It would also be good if you could prevent yourself from loving luxury too much.

Money Number 3

3s could also be lucky when it comes to finances because they have the so-called money vibration. The problem though is that 3s don't usually care for their finances because they just buy what they want all the time. This makes it hard for them to save up for the rainy days, and they might even find themselves in debt or short of funds, even if this could actually be prevented.

The good news is, they can easily pull themselves out of debt, too. They just need to be able to learn from their mistakes.

Money Number 4

Though not really meant to be poor, 4s have to work extremely hard just to gain financial stability. In fact, nothing actually comes easily for him, so most of his life, he'd really be persevering.

However, with enough discipline and control, 4 might be able to grow enough money, especially if he involves himself in the stock market or other kinds of investments. This way, he won't be poverty-stricken for life, and he would be able to take care of his health, too.

Money Number 5

5s are naturally good with business, are organized and focused, and that's why it's easy for them to take care of their finances.

With their streak of philanthropy, they could have people who will help them with their every need, and who would respect their decisions especially when it comes to work and business. 5s believe that money should be given when need be, and that's why it's also easy for money to come back to them. It's almost always replenished. This is because the universe rewards them for their good deeds!

Money Number 6

6 is a symbol of provision and abundance. Material things aren't hard for them to achieve, and these include money. These people also often inherit family wealth, or are given money without them asking for it.

These people also often receive gifts and recognition, and more often than not, succeed in whatever they put their minds to. They mostly never have to worry about cash flow, and their finances just stay stable for all time—no drastic highs or lows!

Money Number 7

Another number that's prone to financial problems is number 7. They have almost the same vibrations as number 2, and are mostly able to gain prosperity in other aspects of life, except for finances.

However, when they work hard to achieve what they want, money comes next. They should then learn how to care for their finances, and not use them for every single thing they want. They also shouldn't hoard material things too much.

Money Number 8

8 is also a symbol of wealth. However, the problem is that it may also be equal to extreme losses. Sometimes, 8s have the tendency to spend money just so they'd be forced to make money again, and of course, this is something that's really not helpful.

They often have extremely expensive lifestyles and find it hard to live by their means, and that's why they're often left in a pool of debt.

Money Number 9

9s easily attract money and are often said to have the "Midas Touch".

However, they might also live expensive lifestyles, or are anxious when they have no money in their pockets. Like 8s, they have the tendency to spend so they'd be motivated to work harder and gain money.

Being compassionate, they're also people who are quite philanthropic. They'd help others even when there's only little left for them, and that's why they also find it hard to save up.

CHAPTER 6

Motivation Number—How Numbers Motivate You

Some people are easily motivated while others just need that little extra push. This so happens because we all have different motivation numbers. Your motivation number also explains why you're inclined to do certain things, and why you feel good some place, when you don't feel good in the other.

Getting the Motivation Number could be tricky. This involves all the letters of your full name, adding up the numbers, and then adding more until you get either 1 to 9 or 11 or 22.

1	2	3	4	5	6	7	8	9
A	B	C	D	E	F	G	H	I
J	K	L	M	N	O	P	Q	R
S	T	U	V	W	X	Y	Z	

http://www.astralaspects.biz/images/page/num_table_pythag.gif

The chart above shows the letters that fall under numbers 1 to 9. Now, all you have to do is chart your name and see where it falls. Let's use the name Sam Smith for example.

S	A	M		S	M	I	T	H
	1					9		

1+9 = 10
1+0 = 1

http://www.astralaspects.biz/images/page/num_samsmith_motivation.gif

For the name SAM SMITH, you have:

S = 1

A = 1

M = 4

S = 1

M = 4

I = 9

T = 2

H = 8

When you add all that up, you'll get 30.

30 = 3 + 0 = 3

This means Sam Smith's Motivation Number is 3! This might be tricky for long names, but hey, if you'd learn more about yourself, then why not?

Motivation Numbers

Now, let's try to explain these motivation numbers more.

1: The Pioneer Spirit

1s are motivated to be independent, goal-oriented, and creative. They believe they have to be visible in the things they are doing or that are related to them for them to feel right about themselves.

1s want to get involved in a lot of things as they naturally have lots of interests and are constantly looking for opportunities that could make their lives better. They know they are leaders, and when they use this for the good, they're able to bring a lot of great things into their lives.

1s are also not so emotional, which is why they can easily motivate themselves even when they fall. This means they want to show others that they can stand on their own two feet, and that they are responsible for their actions.

2: The Diplomatic Spirit

2s are motivated to have this sense of diplomacy and cooperation around him, and that's why he always wants to be part of a team. This way, he feels like he could really tap into the best of himself, instead of just being in the background.

However, when things don't go their way, especially when it comes to friendship or marriage, they find it hard to remind themselves that things could actually be okay again. They could be easily hurt, and take time to acknowledge that life isn't always a bed of roses.

But, when projects are handed their way during that time, they feel like they're actually meant to do something good—and they take it with their both hands.

3: The Joyful Spirit

Motivation isn't a problem for 3s because they have joyful spirits. The joy of living is literally what motivates them. They like being around humorous, fun-loving people, and their joyful spirit also makes them easily noticed wherever they go.

Communication is one of their great skills. The fact that they can talk to people and make them listen make them motivated in life. They often love conversing with others and usually have interesting things to say. They express themselves by writing, speaking up, singing, or joining conferences.

4: The Conscientious Spirit

What motivates 4s are structure and stability in their lives. This means everything must go according to plan or else they'll feel like something is wrong and that they have no idea what to do with their lives.

They are quite the kind of people who remember everything. They're the kinds of people who'd like others to see that if you plan and work hard enough, you'll be able to live the kind of life you want. It's not that they'd impose this, but for them, it's enough that people see they're not just wasting their lives.

5: The Adventurer

5s are motivated by fun and adventure. They're motivated by the free world, and everything that's beautiful in it. They're some of the happiest people because they appreciate whatever is around them, but are not quite adept when it comes to relationships.

They have to remember that their desire for freedom should not be destructive, but rather constructive, and they should also remember not everyone are free thinkers. They are also motivated when they get to realize that there are consequences to every action, and that by being free spirits, they could remain responsible, too.

6: The Family Oriented Spirit

6s are motivated by balance, loyalty, harmony, and responsibility, especially in familial settings. They are naturally loving and affectionate and are more motivated when the people around them are, too.

It's important for them to help others see beauty, and let others appreciate diplomacy the way they do. If not, they become a bit frustrated.

It's also good for them to be around beautiful things. Aesthetics move them, and are somewhat part of their genetic makeup. They are also profoundly emotional and understanding.

7: The Solitary Spirit

These are people who are motivated by contemplation, solitude, and the need to reflect about their lives every once in a while. Even if they are surrounded by people, they still begin to be alone in their minds, which make them different from those around them.

The thing about them is that no one really knows them. They are so mysterious and they actually like it that way. Sometimes, though, they find it hard to express themselves, even to those closest to them, and this says a lot about how bad they feel and how this makes them somewhat depressed at times.

Having found wisdom in their lives motivate them to do better again.

8: The Entrepreneurial Spirit

These are people who have high desires for abundance and power, and are motivated by money, and a position of power. It's easy for them to take over big events, and can even bring joy and fulfillment in their own lives.

In short, it's important for them to be able to find their "place" in life, and that it should be somewhere where they could really express themselves and show others what they can do.

They also know that they are spiritual beings and that their bodies are just vessels. However, it's important that they prevent themselves from being judgmental, and that they should learn to save up to provide for themselves and their future families. This would motivate them even more.

9: The Philanthropic Spirit

Philanthropy and Altruism motivate 9s. They have big hearts and open arms and have somehow mastered what unconditional love is like. They have acquired high levels of spirituality in their past lives and that's why they're also in this Zen mode.

However, there are times when life really could be full of drama and challenges and this actually gets to them and shakes them to the core. Sometimes, they feel like they're doing their best and yet, it's not enough so they fall into the pits of depression.

But, it also doesn't take long for them to bounce back. They believe that while things do not make perfect sense now, they will in the long run. They may be their own biggest critics, but they are their biggest motivators, too!

CHAPTER 7

Hidden Passion Numbers—What They Say about Talents

Finally, it's time to learn about your Hidden Passion Numbers, and what they say about your talents!

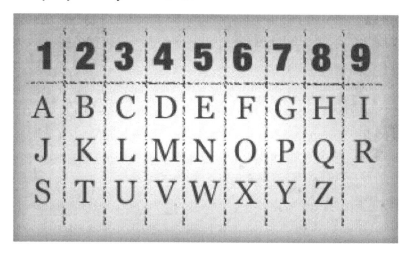

http://gfx.tarot.com/images/numerology-site/pythagorean-chart-300x175.jpg

The thing about this number is that it should be the single digit that occurs the most in your name. It might be a bit tricky, but we could use Tom Cruise's real name, Thomas Cruise Mapother as an example.

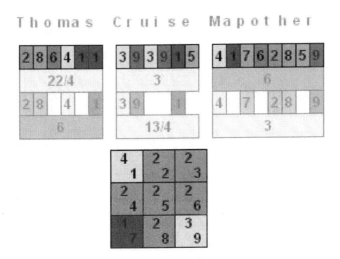

http://gfx.tarot.com/images/numerology-site/cruise-karmic-hidden-passion.jpg

The chart above shows that Tom Cruise has 1 as his prevalent number because there are 4 letters in his name that fall under 1. This is followed by 2 letters under 2, two under 3, and so on.

In short, his Hidden Passion Number is 1.

Try it, and learn more about the said hidden passion numbers below!

Hidden Passion Numbers

Hidden Passion Number 1

1s could be great politicians, actors, or athletes because they are natural leaders, and are born warriors. They have survived many obstacles even in their past lives!

They also have a strong desire to be seen and to stand out. They are motivated to accomplish things, and to be successful and that's why they try to learn a lot of things to enhance their intellect and skills.

Although not that confident early in life, they could fight the shyness and emerge victorious!

Hidden Passion Number 2

2s could be successful anywhere in life because they're amazing followers. They are intuitive, sensitive, and considerate, and always have to have peace around them. They won't do anything to annoy their bosses or co-workers, and are actually eager to learn!

Another great thing about them is that they are committed. They may not be naturally talented, sure, but they're committed to doing their best to improve themselves, which makes them one of the pillars wherever they may be or whatever they may be doing in life.

Hidden Passion Number 3

3s could be great painters, actors, or artists of any kind. They love to socialize, and they love life for what it is. They can easily see its beauty, and are inclined to fantasize especially when times are dull. This way, they don't get bored and they get to stay happy no matter what happens in their lives.

They may sometimes be scatter-brained, but it's also easy for them to get back up and inspire others because they're fun-loving, entertaining individuals!

Hidden Passion Number 4

4s could be great businessmen or leaders because they're the most systematic and organized of all numbers. They also have a great sense of self-discipline and perseverance, which makes it easy for them to do their best in life.

However, a sense of security is important for them so they need to find careers where they could grow, and where they wouldn't have to move to and fro. Their sound judgment makes it easy for them to find a job that they like and be good at it.

Hidden Passion Number 5

5s may be great as diplomats, tour guides, stewardesses, pilots, fashion experts—or just about any job where they could move around a lot and see various parts of the world. They are free spirits who are great with words and languages, but may also be impulsive and sensual.

5s always love to satisfy their senses, so they have to be careful about being overly indulgent in sex, drugs, coffee, food, or a terrible lifestyle. However, their sense of humor and resiliency saves them each time, but may also make it easy for them to leave projects uncompleted and wander from one job to the other.

Hidden Passion Number 6

6s love to care for others, so it might be good if they'd take jobs in the caregiving, nursing, or teaching industries.

They're so responsible that, sometimes, people tend to take advantage of them. They might also be overly self-righteous or idealistic, but otherwise, they are great in everything they do.

Hidden Passion Number 7

Meanwhile, 7s are highly intuitive and motivated and are fast learners. It's good for them to be psychologists, counselors, or writers because they are highly contemplative and are drawn to the metaphysical and philosophical aspects of life.

Sometimes, though, they tend to be cynical and melancholic. But once they get out of their rut, they become some of the most successful people around.

Hidden Passion Number 8

8s are said to be born managers because they are quite the organized kind. But whatever they take on in life, they can do their best because they are eager to please, and always want to have money and that position of power. Their subordinates easily like them, too, so work becomes easy for them.

They are also great judges of character, and always feel that they have to be rewarded for being hard workers and great family men.

Hidden Passion Number 9

Lastly, 9s are some of the most creative people around, and could take jobs in the artistic and writing fields. They might also be good speakers and counselors because they are naturally warm and compassionate, and are considered to be creative geniuses.

They may sometimes be hypersensitive and emotional, but when they're at their best, they really are some of the most responsible and amazing people around.

CHAPTER 8

Numerology and Its Connection to Astrology and Tarot

Somehow, Numerology is also linked to Astrology and Tarot, which also influence how numbers work in your life. For this, you have to make use of your Birth Path Numbers, as seen in the second chapter of this book.

Here's what you need to know:

1: Mercury and the Magician

1 is associated with Mercury in Astrology, also known as the planet of the mind, and of the mouth—adding to the fact that if your number is 1, then you are this being who has primal force. Mercury is also known to be the link to nebulous ideas—ideas that are yet to be tangible, and that you need to wake your mind up to understand.

Apart from Mercury, the number 1 is also associated with The Magician in Tarot. The Magician is known to perform "hands-on magic", which means that he feels a certain allegiance between himself, heaven, and earth.

With those associations, and if 1 is your number, you have to remember that you should be the first person to trust yourself, because if you wouldn't do so, no one else will. You also have to learn to be curious, open up your mind, and think like a scientist—open to new ideas, and open to failure, but also having the resolve to rise up again. Explore; be someone who learns more about the world, and is not afraid to try new things. Never hold yourself back for you are someone who's capable of doing lots of great things in the world.

2: The Moon and the High Priestess

In Astrology, this number is associated with the moon. This means that while you are all-knowing, and incredibly smart, chances are, you also have more emotional problems than some of the numbers on the list. You may also have problems regarding feeling safe and secure at some points in your life.

Meanwhile, number 2 is also associated with the High Priestess, one of the most popular characters in Tarot. The High Priestess in your number means that you have to learn how to be more spiritual, though not exactly religious. You have to try learning about Supreme Beings, and just the thought that we are never really alone in this world. You have to learn how to cooperate with the spirit so that you would also be able to retreat and find some serenity during times when you feel so lost, and feel like your whole world is caving in. In short, finding a spiritual routine is something that can truly improve your life.

3: Venus and the Empress

The Creative Child is associated with Venus in Astrology, also known as the planet of the inner world. This is more about your inner self, rather than the person, or the "you" that you are trying to show the world. This also affects your emotional tendencies, and shows that you have this certain peace between here, and to whatever comes next.

In Tarot, number 3 is associated with what is known as The Empress. The Empress is a sign that says you should not be so hard on yourself—because the people around you probably already are. While there are times when your actions may not provide favorable outcomes, it doesn't mean that you have to totally berate yourself, and make yourself feel terrible. What you should do, then, is plan your course of action, and trust your good senses. Know what you are good at, and play with those, rather than critique yourself for what you're not a master of. Know how to carry out your responsibilities well, and know how to be accountable for your own actions, instead of always depending on others, or blaming them for your wrongdoings.

You also have to be more caring; more showy of how you feel, instead of just trying to hide everything in for fear of being judged. Be more understanding of the struggles and needs of others and you'll feel a whole lot lighter inside.

4: Aries and the Emperor

Meanwhile, the fourth sign is connected with Aries in Astrology. This is why if this is your number, you may have a bold, fiery, and fearless spirit. Aries is also known to be the most action-oriented sign, which means that you might also be highly competitive. You won't have much of a hard time when it comes to getting your voice heard because you are naturally already impossible to ignore, and have the power when it comes to making speeches. The only problem is that you might be too adamant with your beliefs that you refuse to listen to anyone else.

In Tarot, 4 is associated with the Emperor. Basically, this means that you are a natural healer, and that you are actually brighter, and smarter than you think. You then need to have faith in your own power and creativity, and you have to learn not to doubt yourself, but not to be too aggressive while doing so. Be curious and open-minded, and just learn that you actually have ingenious timing that can help you sail through life.

5: Taurus and the Hierophant

Next up is number 5, which in Astrology is related with Taurus. Seemingly stubborn, those under this sign only need to be surrounded by the great, otherwise known as the finer things in life, to be able to succeed. Being under this sign means that you probably also are practical, sensible, and stable, love food, material possessions, and even sex. The problem, though, is that you may tend to be the kind of person who cannot deal with not getting what he wants. The good thing, though, is that you also do not easily give up, and you know how important your passions are to help you glide through life.

When it comes to Tarot, the number 5 is associated with the Hierophant, also known as a master of natural law and practical lessons; someone who apparently knows the link between the earth and the heavens. You may find that in times of adversities in life, you'll be able to survive better when you begin to harmonize your talents or skills with what you already have, or how your lifestyle is like. You also have the tendency to be meticulous, and if you aren't already, then it's recommended that you try being that way. You also should be open-minded about learning more, because whatever you learn are things you can use to help you get through life, especially if these are about where you currently live. Broaden your experiences in life and you will gain respect and admiration from your peers, and never forget to concentrate on your goals, and on whatever you have to do in life.

6: Gemini and the Lovers

Number 6 is related to Gemini in Astrology, more popularly known as the "twins". You probably are a born communicator, and you do know how to speak your mind well. Geminis are partly brainy, but could also be scatterbrained, and this is why you have to learn how to make use of introspection, and numerology to help yourself feel better. However, once you learn to know yourself better, you can be one of the funniest, most interesting people around. You might also be quite flirty, and could be someone who tries to use his charm to get his way, or make his way out of certain things. One thing that you do have to remember, though, is that you have to learn how to slow down and calm your mind so that you won't easily be distracted of what's happening in your life.

In Tarot, this number is associated with The Lovers, which also says a lot about how you choose a partner in life. What this means, though, is that whoever you choose to be intimate with, you should be fully committed. This is also why you have to "study your options" first so you'd be sure that you're with the right person, especially if a long-term relationship is in your mind. Be mindful of the choices you'll make, especially if you know they're going to bring forth some discontent. Always learn to stick with your choice, and don't be too fickle-minded—or you just may hurt yourself and some people, too.

7: Cancer and the Chariot

The Number 7 is associated with the Cancer sign in Astrology. This means that you have the tendency to be quite sensitive, mostly because you are ruled by the emotional moon. While you have this tough exterior, you may also be the kind of person who keeps his feelings hidden just to avoid getting hurt, which may also mean that you're not really living life to the fullest, and thus, you're often said to be "crabby". This could be changed, though, when you meet someone—or even a group of friends—who really gets you for who you are, and whom you can be completely honest with. You may also be naturally protective, but at the same time, you may have crazy mood swings that you have to try to prevent from happening, if you can. Try to manage and process these feelings first before reacting or you may just overreact.

Meanwhile, when it comes to the Tarot, this sign is connected to the Chariot, or someone who parades himself as a "hero" along the streets. What you have to understand is that even though you may be "on top" now, it doesn't necessarily mean that it's what's going to happen forever. Therefore, you have to learn how to be open to changes, and understand that life isn't always a constant thing. Learn how to be receptive to the new people in your life, as well. This way, you can "travel light", and just allow yourself to glide through life better.

8: Leo and Strength

Next up is number 8, which in Astrology is associated with the Leo sign. Leo stands for the Lion, which means that you could be quite fiery, and are someone who cannot easily be ignored. You are quite charming, and also has the love for drama, and naturally has a warm spirit, and is quite hospitable. You are an actionable person—you don't like to just sit around and do nothing, and you often make sure that you do what you can to live life well. However, you could be quite attention-seeking, arrogant, and may be keen on throwing temper tantrums. This is why it is recommended that you try to pay attention to the people and the events happening around you, and to be less dominating than you actually are, so you can relate to people more.

In Tarot, this number is related to Strength, which determines your nature in its most primal form. You could be quite persuasive, especially when it comes to what you want in life. You also have to learn to distinguish your ego from your true self, and you should separate enlightened wisdom from self-interest. Have some integrity so you could influence others in the right manner, so that this way, you will succeed with whatever you have in mind, as long as it is good, of course!

9: Virgo and the Hermit

The Number 9 is related to Virgo in Astrology. Also known as the Virgin, this means that you can be quite analytical, detail-oriented, and ultimately hardworking, and you kind of get to see what's wrong with certain people or with their environments right away. However, the problem is that when some people start critiquing you, you do not take to it too lightly, and you may easily turn your back on them when this happens. Therefore, you have to try to lessen the perfectionism and just try to be a realist—after all, no one is perfect, and it's always best to just do your best, instead of seeking to be "perfect" and destroying everything you have put your heart and soul into before.

In Tarot, this number is associated with the Hermit. This means that you're able to recognize those people who could teach you a thing or two about life—otherwise known as your life teachers or mentors. You are the kind of person who gains wisdom from your experiences in life, and from the people you meet, and who make an impact in your life. One thing you have to remember, though, is that you have to try to think things through, and that you have to be careful of the way you think, as well. This way, you get to understand the larger things in life, and learn to see the bigger picture. You also need alone time, so do not be scared to tell people that you need to be alone for a while, think, and then just get your ducks in a row.

CHAPTER 9

Double Digit Numbers

In Numerology, there are also double digit numbers. For example, your Birth Path number is 9. 9 is the result of 7 + 2 (72), 6 + 3 (63), 4 + 5 (45), 8 + 1 (81), and all its other variations. Therefore, even if your birth path number could already say a lot about you, there are different versions of numbers that make it up—which means there are also underlying characteristics that are dictated by each double digit number, and now, you'll get to learn more about them.

A simple exercise to determine your double digit number is to reduce your birthday to double digits. For example, your birthday is 10-18-1988, you should add the numbers 1 + 0 + 1 + 9 + 1 + 9 + 8 + 8 = 36. 36 is then your double digit number. These numbers could also be anything from 10 to 99!

How do these double digit numbers affect your life, then? Read on, and find out!

10

10 is known to enhance all the qualities that 1 has. If this is your double-digit number, it denotes that you are streamlined for success, and that you are focused, and are a natural leader. One thing about this number is that you're known to be such a go-getter—like you're someone who won't stop until you get what you want, which also makes others feel like you're such a domineering force.

11

11 is known to be the most intuitive number. It is deemed to be the channel to the subconscious, and is known to represent vision. It means

that you may rely more on insight than on rational thought, which might not be helpful in extremely logical situations. You may also tend to be nervous, sensitive, impractical, and shy, but are energetic when the situation calls for it.

Since 2 is the all-knowing, it means that 11 heightens those things with proper inspiration, leadership values, and amazing charisma. This number has duality in its core, which helps you realize that you may also be guilty in creating your own phobias and fears, as a means to punish yourself at times when you feel like life isn't good, or that your efforts are not getting you anywhere. You often walk the edge between greatness and self-destruction, and this is why you have to be mindful of what you are doing, and find time to reflect and ask yourself certain questions every once in a while. To make sure that you use this number the right way, you should get to know your spirit and use your intuition for the good of people. Peace is not found in logic, but may be found in faith, so you have to try to get some sense of responsibility and be faithful to something.

12

12 is unconventional and highly creative. This number mostly just represents your own interests, and does not care too much about many other things.

13

13 is a Karmic Debt Number. This means that when you're handed a task, no matter what it is, you'd do everything you can to accomplish the said task in the right manner and time. You'd often find a way to overcome the obstacles that come your way, even if you notice that some of them are happening over and over again. The problem is that some people with this number tend to be lazy, especially when it comes to money matters—and yet, they still expect to succeed in life. What you have to remember is that perseverance matters, and when you persevere, success will come your way—no matter how long. In

fact, most athletes, businessmen, and artists have 13 as their karmic number.

In order to make sure that you get positive karma out of this number, you should be able to focus on your main goals. Do not try to distribute your energy to various things that you only like for a moment, and would then get to forget later. You have to learn how to choose the projects that you do in life, and make sure they are in line with what you want to happen. Remember that easy success may just give you regrets later on, so it is so much better to do things that you know would help you in the long run. Make sure that there is some order in your life so you can focus on what you need to concentrate on.

14

14 is quite a complicated number, mostly because it's said to have risen from previous lifetimes, which means you might be the kind of person who has to face so many adversities in life. It means you have to grow a strong backbone to be able to prepare for the many changes and troubles in your life, and that as much as you can, it's best to stay away from things like alcohol, drugs, or any other vices that you may overindulge in. You have to learn how to be modest, and see the silver lining in every dark cloud so that you would not be tempted to get on these vices.

You should learn to be flexible, and understand that life isn't something that will always go your way. In case you struggle, learn to focus on your strengths and on what you can do, instead of on what you can't. When you set your mind and heart to the right things for you, you will feel that life is so much lighter—and you will feel like you can actually make your dreams come true!

15

Those with this number are extremely talented, tolerant, forgiving, and ultimately loving—traits that most people would actually want to have. You could also be quite self-indulgent, and have the tendency to experiment somehow in life, and have the love for adventure and travel, among many things.

16

This number is like the phoenix—it's all about rising up from the ashes; out with the old, in with the new. At times when your ego falls, you will find the strength to stand up from the rubble and bounce back. You also know how to destroy things inside you that deviate you from being the person you are supposed to be, even if at times, it seems like life is giving you so many challenges that may be detrimental to your grand plans in life. For you, there is always time for rebirth, because you can live many lives in your lifetime. You may also be highly intuitive, and because of that, you may have the tendency to look down on others whom you see as people who are not doing their best in life, and when this happens, you may begin to alienate people— which could then bring you lots of loneliness in life. While it is good to know who the bad weeds are, it does not necessarily mean that you have to let go of every person in your life, leaving you with none. You can then sail through life better by learning to place your faith on a Supreme Being, or just improving your spirituality any way you can.

17

This number is a reflection of balance, substance, emotional growth, and faith. On the other hand, it also means that you may have the tendency to be bankrupt, deal with financial problems, and may struggle to remain true to your moral values.

18

This is about being involved in international affairs or businesses. It also helps you draw the line between selfishness and idealism, and more often than not, this may mean that there is a lack of spiritual effort from you.

19

This number means that you are someone who is capable of learning how to use power properly, which also means that you're not the type of person who would compromise your integrity just so people would look up to you. It's not like you to abuse your power just to gain the attention of others. You have such a strong personality, so strong, in fact, that sometimes, people tend to just leave you alone, thinking that you do not need help of any sort, which is why you are often left to fend for yourself.

Another problem is that you could be quite stubborn. You hate listening to others, so you do not listen, even if you already need help—which also means that you have the tendency to alienate people and become a recluse. If you do not accept the fact that you need love in your life, you may live a very lonely life, so while it's good that you're trying to stand on your own, you should realize that you still need people in your life—you need to have a deep connection even with just a small number of people to feel better about who and what you are in life, and with whatever it is that you are doing.

20

20s are overly sensitive, vulnerable, intuitive, and may not take criticism lightly. You may show cowardice or weaknesses in times of adversities, and you may also have lots of emotional problems, too.

21

This number is unconventional and highly creative. This number mostly just represents your own interests, and does not care too much about many other things.

22

22 is a Master Number that is also quite powerful, just like number 11, but is oftentimes more successful than 11. It means that you may rely

more on insight than on rational thought, which might not be helpful in extremely logical situations. You may also tend to be nervous, sensitive, impractical, and shy, but are energetic when the situation calls for it. This number has duality in its core, which helps you realize that you may also be guilty of creating your own phobias and fears, as a means to punish yourself at times when you feel like life isn't good, or that your efforts are not doing anything to improve your condition. You often walk the edge between greatness and self-destruction, and this is why you have to be mindful of what you are doing, and find time to reflect and ask yourself certain questions every once in a while. To make sure that you use this number the right way, you should get to know your spirit and use your intuition for the good of people. Peace is not found in logic, but may be found in faith, so you have to try to get some sense of responsibility and be faithful to something.

23

23 is a symbol of someone who tries to fight for freedom, and is passionate with what he or she is doing in life. The problem is that you may sometimes be unrealistic, and may have the tendency to be a quitter, but when you like what you are doing, you will stand by it— and the causes that are connected to it, too!

24

24 has a counseling, peaceful nature—making you the mother hen of your group. You may have a passion for dance and music, and other forms of art, but may also have problems with your relationships, ultimately leading to divorce and other forms of struggles.

25

This number denotes spiritual leadership, and may have the tendency to join many endeavors, but has problems sharing his or her thoughts and feelings.

26

This number has a lot to do with management and business, and one could often be such a workaholic, but is a good strategist. If this is your number, you just have to be mindful of being more organized in your affairs, or else, you may encounter a lot of problems.

27

This number has a lot to do with volunteerism and counseling. If this is your number, you may also have the tendency to be an artist, and may have the chance to inherit certain things in life. You might be quite successful, too. You have to avoid being extremely narrow-minded or rigid, and learn to open up your mind to various things in life—because there really are a lot of things you can learn about in this world.

28

If this is your double-digit number, it denotes that you are streamlined for success, and that you are focused, and are a natural leader. One thing about this number is that you're known to be such a go-getter—like you're someone who won't stop until you get what you want, which also makes others feel like you're such a domineering force.

29

This is almost the same as 11, but the difference is that you should learn how to deal with things that make you feel pressured. You have to learn how not to pressure yourself too much so that you wouldn't crack under pressure, and so you would not waste your potential, but still enjoy a lot of great things in life. You can also be more social, or more serious, depending on what you choose.

30

This denotes the fact that you can be quite creative, and a great communicator. However, while you are someone who adapts the "laughter is the best medicine" paradigm, you may also be quite superficial, and at times, overbearing. It's like you have this wall between you and people, but you're putting out such a jovial façade that is far from the real you—which could be an act that's too tiring, altogether.

31

This number denotes exuberance, and being extroverted. In fact, you may be the kind of person who gets to have more fun than others, but also have the tendency to cheat or not be ultimately faithful to your partner. Therefore, when you're already committed, make sure that you wouldn't do anything that could ruin the relationship—especially if it is a deliberate action.

32

This is the same as number 23, but the difference is that you may have a lot of mood swings, and could experience a lot of emotional ups and downs in your life.

33

33 is also quite an influential number, and is known as the Master Teacher, which could bring your potential to another, better level. You may not have those concrete goals the way some of your peers have, but you do tend to be quite spiritual, and could care for mankind quite well, and are actually devoted to this thought, which is also why a lot of people are impressed by you. You're the kind of person who actually practices what he preaches—you won't tell others not to do certain things when you know you are guilty of doing them yourself. This is also why you are considered such a rare and special person.

34

This denotes spiritual purity and intelligence, is a natural warrior, and is known to be the kind of person who knows how to easily share with others.

35

This is a number that denotes creativity, especially when it comes to business. You could either be a gadget designer, an inventor, or a business adviser of some sorts. You might not be keen on working with others, though, so freelance jobs are recommended for you—so you can also work on your own pace and not be easily pressured.

36

Often deemed as a creative genius, those under this number are quite artistic, but could also have the tendency to be aloof, inhibited, and self-conscious—traits that could make or break you as a person, especially when it comes to your line of work.

37

Those under this number are highly individualistic, and could often be voracious readers. Most of the time, and if you are under this number, you might also have an excellent imagination, although you might also be the kind of person who's messy and disorganized, most of the time.

38

This is a more realistic version of number 11—and more grounded, too. You're quite intuitive, but you are not the type who is going to admit it, for the most part. You may also have loads of phobias, and could be quite successful when it comes to picking, or selling antiques.

39

A person who's under this number is someone who truly loves art, and is someone who often sings or dances. Highly idealistic and jolly, this person might also be someone who has a fear of rejection, or has a hard time dealing with it—same goes for separation, too.

40

This is 4's high octave number, and is systematic, highly organized, and methodical. On the negative side, you may be overly critical of others, and may have so many prejudices that prevent you from finding real friends. You may lack some sense of humor, too.

41

This means you have to grow a strong backbone to be able to prepare for the many changes and troubles in your life, and that as much as you can, it's best to stay away from things like alcohol, drugs, or any other vices that you may overindulge in. You have to learn how to be modest, and see the silver lining in every dark cloud so that you would not be tempted to get on these vices. You should learn to be flexible, and understand that life isn't something that will always go your way. In case you struggle, learn to focus on your strengths and on what you can do, instead of on what you can't. When you set your mind and heart to the right things for you, you will feel that life is so much lighter—and you will feel like you can actually make your dreams come true.

42

If you're under this number, chances are, you are—or have dreams of being—an administrator, or that you have political aspirations. You may also be someone who is quite inferior, and has many frustrations in life.

43

This one means that you have high levels of concentration, but that you could also be quite a perfectionist, and may also prove to be insensitive to most people's needs. Feelings of inferiority may be prevalent, too.

44

This number means that you just might be destined for business, or that you may be eyeing a career in the military, or something close to that. You have great potential in life as you are not just a doer, but a visionary, too.

45

If you're under this number, you might easily be involved in banking, or diplomatic or international institutions. The catch, though, is that you may also be someone who is quite cynical and are not comfortable with yourself.

46

This is another number that denotes leadership, but could also be rude or tactless, but could make up for it with the right amount of confidence.

47

Another Master Number, this one is usually involved in the struggle to find spiritual connections and being down to earth. But, once you get to find that balance, you won't struggle anymore, and you'd be able to live a peaceful, satisfying life—one that you can actually be proud of.

48

Those under this number are planners and visionaries, but could also have such unrealistic dreams in life.

49

This number means that when you're handed a task, no matter what it is, you will do everything you can to accomplish the said task in the right manner and time. You will often find a way to overcome the obstacles that come your way, even if you notice that some of them are happening over and over again. The problem is that some with this number tend to be lazy, especially when it comes to money matters—and yet, they still expect to succeed in life. What you have to remember is that perseverance matters, and when you persevere, success will come your way—no matter how long. In fact, most athletes, businessmen, and artists have 13 as their karmic number.

In order to make sure that you get positive karma out of this number, you should be able to focus on your main goals. Do not try to distribute your energy to various things that you only like for a moment, and would then get to forget later. You have to learn how to choose the projects that you do in life, and make sure they are in line with what you want to happen. Remember that easy success may just give you regrets later on, so it's so much better to do things that you know would help you in the long run. Make sure that there is some order in your life so you can focus on what you need to concentrate on.

50

This is a version of #5 that's considered as "high octave", which means that if this is your number, then you are probably quite versatile and fun-loving, willing to take chances, and are actually open to new ideas. The problem, though, is that more often than not, you may have sexual hang-ups.

51

This is an aggressive and more independent version of 15.

52

This person is creative, intuitive, and sensitive.

53

A verbal, more detail-oriented, creative version of number 35.

54

This person is a less-organized version of number 45, is disciplined, but may have a hard time finishing projects. He may also be quite idealistic, but is a natural dreamer.

55

If this is your number, then you are a person who's extremely fun-loving. While you are naturally outgoing and social, there might also be those moments when you feel extremely sad—even for no reason at all.

56

This one represents balance and sensitivity, and that certain desire for freedom, but also the feeling that you're longing for a family—or just a group of people whom you feel like you belong with.

57

This stands for inventiveness and intelligence, and having the chance to gain so much wisdom in life. If this is your number, then, you might also be unconventional and creative.

58

58 represents success and a full willingness to work. You're the kind of person who can make fast but viable decisions, and is someone

who can easily recognize opportunities. You might also be quite opinionated and dogmatic, somehow.

59

This number represents how you could be quite convincing and persuasive, and is mostly for fundraisers or lawyers. It also represents one's ability to understand diverse cultures and be comfortable with people from all walks of life.

60

This means that you are responsible, caring, and loving, but could also be subservient.

61

This means that you may be someone who often experiences difficulties in relationships, and love, in general. You have a strong need for connection, and having a good group of family and friends. You are secretive, and could also be demanding, but could work great when it comes to careers regarding the Secret Service, law, or research.

62

This number has a lot to do with management and business, and could often be such a workaholic, but is a good strategist. If this is your number, you just have to be mindful of being more organized in your affairs, or else, you may encounter a lot of problems. You may be just a bit sensitive, and might succeed in careers regarding the medical field.

63

This is a less outgoing version of 36, but could be quite promiscuous.

64

This is a creative and less-organized version of 46.

65

If this is your number, then, you will always have a need for freedom and the chance to be your own, even if you are committed, in one way or the other. This number also represents a criminal tendency.

66

This is a sign of financial ups and downs, but could be quite generous to a fault. This also means that you are loving and kind, and that you will find a way to be successful even if sometimes, you feel like you don't like yourself too much.

67

This is a sign of creativity and analytical intelligence, which is why you might find yourself successful in the fields of mathematics, and inventions.

68

This is a sign that you have a keen eye for business and that you might be quite successful with it. You have an amazing sense of humor—but can be quite sensitive, too.

69

69 is a sign of being self-sacrificing. You might lean towards environmentalism or politics, teaching, or medicine, and could also be quite creative.

70

This signifies that you might be a "hermit". You are a seeker of truth, and because you often try to look for depth in the things in your life, then it also means that you might be quite lonely. You often tend to lose touch with the "material world". You're also quite original and intelligent, and is extremely eccentric.

71

This is a lonelier and less authoritative version of number 17.

72

This one is an excellent conversationalist and is the voracious reader type.

73

If this is your number, then, you might be fond of spending a lot of time alone—even working alone.

74

Another Master Number, this one is usually involved in the struggle to find spiritual connections and being down to earth. But, once you get to find that balance, you won't struggle anymore, and you'd be able to live a peaceful, satisfying life—one that you can actually be proud of.

75

A more creative and less analytical version of 57.

76

This means you could easily be involved in management, which might also mean you're prone to religious fanaticism and dogmatism. However, you also have this great ability of turning your ideas into reality, as well.

77

This is known to be the most inventive and possibly the most intelligent of all numbers. This is also telling of how spiritually wise you are.

78

This is all about material versus spiritual struggle, and is also about making and losing fortunes.

79

This might mean that you could be a political or spiritual leader, but that you could be quite self-righteous and overbearing.

80

If this is your number, then you probably have an eye for business, or the military. You might be quite extroverted and independent, but may often have this lack of independence, which definitely isn't good at all.

81

This is a more money-oriented version of number 18, but is also someone who lacks spiritual wisdom and understanding. You have to try to control your mood swings and anger if this is your number because you have the tendency to be violent.

82

This denotes courage and strong leadership. Somehow, it also means that you are quite the survivor, but because you are strong-willed and independent, you may have a hard time keeping relationships, even marriage. If you are this person, then you probably don't like to be committed, or would rather prefer to be alone.

83

A more business-oriented version of 38.

84

This is a less-organized version of 48, and is actually a visionary.

85

This could be a bullish or more masculine version of 58.

86

If this is your number, then, you are self-oriented or self-aware, but could be quite self-indulgent or irresponsible.

87

This is a more money-savvy and practical version of 78, but also has that need to drive balance between material and spiritual needs.

88

If this is your number then you are someone who's full of contradictions. You're smart and business-savvy, but you may not know how to handle relationships well, and you may also find it hard to be alone—even for a short period of time!

89

Aristocracy may rule your life if this is your double digit number, or being a "person of the world"—someone who loves life and all the great and grand things in it.

90

If this is your number then you are humble and self-sacrificing, and you could easily get and feel religious fervor. While you may tend to be aloof, it doesn't really hurt your character because people are still drawn to you.

91

If this is your number, then you're part of the lucky bunch because you easily notice that you have lots of successes in your career, as well as with your finances. You're also opinionated and eccentric, as well.

92

This means you have great concern for mankind, and could be altruistic, too.

93

This means that you might be good with gardens and landscaping, and that you are quite creative—but have problems with commitment.

94

This is another version of 49, and is the type who doesn't take changes too lightly, and is comfortable with travel.

95

This is an impractical and dreamy version of number 59—and is someone who loves to travel.

96

This is a self-sacrificing version of 69 and is someone who's family-oriented, and loves the community, his family, and friends.

97

This is a more sensitive version of number 79.

98

If this is your number then you probably are an idealist and that you may also be indifferent. This also means that you have a hard time showing emotions, or that you may not be easily understood by others.

99

Finally, the number 99 represents artistic genius. However, if this is your number then you might also be someone who's often the target of gossip. It can also bring lots of possessiveness and jealousy to your relationships.

CHAPTER 10

Balance Numbers—How They Give Balance and Coordination to Your Life

And then of course, there are also Balance Numbers. Balance Numbers have this minor—but definitely unforgettable—influence in your life. This is because balance numbers provide you with guidance during those times when you feel like you don't know how to deal with what's going on in your life, and your main course of action is to withdraw from life.

When you withdraw from life, and just try to stay away from mostly anyone or anything—especially for long periods of time—it means that you need someone to talk to, or at least, a way for you to understand what's going on inside you. This also goes for those times when you're dealing with emotional breakdowns, or when you just want to go ahead and scream.

With the help of balance numbers, you get to pacify yourself better, and you also get to help yourself out of trouble.

To get your balance number, just add the numerical values of your initials—your first, middle, and last, and then reduce that to a single digit. You could get numerical values from the image (page 78):

http://gfx.tarot.com/images/numerology-site/pythagorean-chart-300x175.jpg

So, for example, your name is Kimberly Alison Spears, your initials are K (2), A (1), and S (1). Add 2 + 1 + 1, and you'd get the result of 4, which means that 4 is your Balance Number.

Here's what you need to know about each balance number:

Balance Number 1

If 1 is your balance number then it means that you have to learn to draw strength from yourself—within yourself. However, you might also find it helpful to share your story and your feelings with family and friends—just learn to strike the balance between the two.

If you're more of the loner type and tend to hold everything in, know that there are still people you can trust. When you open your ears, and mind, and heart to advice, you might just learn more about what's happening, as well as the world around you. This way, you can also find new approaches to certain problems. You need to stay creative, courageous, and strong, and you'll surely find your way out of any problem.

Balance Number 2

If this is your balance number then you have to learn how to make use of diplomacy and tact to resolve things. Do not be too tactless, and do not be over sensitive. Learn how to put a balance in your emotions and learn to not be swayed so much. You have to understand that when you begin to live harmoniously in the world, then that's when you begin to find peace and wisdom in your life.

Think about whatever problems you're facing. Be open to other people's advice, and learn to not escape from your problems—escape is just a defense mechanism and isn't a solution. In fact, you have it within you to find solutions to whatever it is that's bugging you or people you know—make use of that. Also, learn to not make mountains out of molehills—don't make a big deal out of simple things.

Balance Number 3

You know what? You're a naturally charming person, and your charm is something you have to learn to use for your benefit. The issue is that when faced with a problem, you tend to be overly emotional, and this clouds the way you see things, as well as your judgment. Try to be objective, not subjective. Look at the bigger picture and see things for what they really are. Always be open to more than one option so that whatever you decide on would provide the right impact to your life, and to the people around you, too. Learn to be optimistic and lighthearted—life is short, after all, and it wouldn't be right to just spend your whole life hating anything and anyone.

Balance Number 4

Just like number three, you need to open your eyes some more. You may have the tendency to be cynical, but the reason why certain problems keep on happening is mostly because you don't tend to lose your fear from what has happened in the past. Be more lighthearted and try to open up your heart and you'll realize that life actually isn't that bad, and that there is a way out of your problems in life.

Another thing that you should remember is that you have to learn how to compromise because once you do, you'll realize that your sense of justice would be elevated to another level. Learn to see life through another person's eyes; learn to walk in their shoes and you would understand a lot more things about life. Remember that there are a lot of angles to one thing—don't be focused on just one thing alone.

Balance Number 5

If your balance number is 5, then, you have to learn to focus on the problem itself and not on whatever's surrounding it. It's also important to help yourself realize that defense mechanisms and other forms of comfort—whether food, alcohol, or drugs—would not do you any good, and could even provide you with more problems. What you have to do now is find a quiet place—a place where you can think, and just reflect on the problem—so that a proper solution can come to you.

Balance Number 6

Remember that it is natural for you to be understanding of others, and what happens in their lives. It is now your job to show yourself that same kindness. It might seem easy to just rely on the people in your life to help you solve those problems, but the better thing would be to just go talk to them, help them provide you with solace, but do not expect them to solve all your problems for you. That is something you have to do yourself. Remember that everything that happens in life is something that you're also remotely responsible for—which means that you have it in you to solve them, too. Be accountable for your actions.

Balance Number 7

It's so easy for you to "escape" from your problems, in one way or the other. Sometimes, you tend to just retreat into yourself without solving the problem itself. You have to learn how to stay in the world—even if you know that you've got to face your demons. Facing your demons while still trying to live life is something so courageous. Learn to confront yourself so you can deal with the issues at hand, and learn how not to be too emotional when dealing with things.

Balance Number 8

You have a means to create some sense of balance in your life, especially when it comes to making sense of emotional issues, so always remember that. However, you also have the tendency to be manipulative—try to prevent that from happening by being responsible for your actions; having some accountability. Take note that you are smart enough to be a natural leader—and you can lead your life where you want it to go. When dealing with other people, do not force them to just see things your way—remember that everyone deals with things differently. Learn to show respect.

Balance Number 9

Your main issue in life is that you often fail to empathize with others, but the thing is it is natural for you to be understanding of things and what's happening with the world—that is something you could use for your benefit. Learn to avoid being aloof, and learn to find answers within yourself. You just might be surprised.

CHAPTER 11

Cornerstone, Capstone, Key, and First Vowel in Numerology

Finally, it's time to learn about how the letters in your name would affect your life. There are letters that are more important than the rest.

For this, you can make use of the chart in the earlier chapter—regarding numerical values of letters, and see the triangle below as an example:

http://www.decoz.com/images/CornerCapKey.gif

Cornerstone

On the bottom left part is the Cornerstone, or the letter of your first name. For example, if your name is Adam, then A = 1 (as seen on the image in an earlier chapter). The Cornerstone is something that provides light on your entire personality—on who you really are as a person.

Capstone

Then, on the bottom right corner is the Capstone, or the last letter of your name. This demonstrates the way ideas play out in your head, and the way you see things, as a whole. This shows how you can start and end projects.

Key / First Vowel

Finally, on top is the key, also known as the first vowel (A, E, I, O, U) of your name. This denotes your deepest urges, dreams, fears, and goals. It denotes what drives you—what makes you who you are.

Here are the meanings of the letters in your name:

A

A is all about being your own person; being self-seeking, rather than being easily influenced. It's not easy for you to change your mind—you have your own free will. You are also a natural and purposeful leader.

B

B means that you could be quite introverted but you still know how to relate to the world and be compassionate and loving. You always aim for peace and serenity in your life, and are actually very loyal—and open-minded, too!

C

This means that you easily wear your heart on your sleeve, and that you are headstrong when it comes to emotional issues. You are witty, and you know how to express yourself clearly. You are also upbeat and quite outspoken.

D

The D in your name means that you are pragmatic and grounded, and that you always want to get things done. You also know how to get things done because you have your own "system" for mostly everything—just be careful to still open up your mind and not be too stubborn.

E

E means that you are authentic. You might also be the type who's sensual and fun-loving and are just in love with life—even with love! You are the life of the party and are quite outgoing, and you are also someone who's hard to fool, as well!

F

You are a good host, are responsible, and nurturing. You could be maternal, or like the mother hen of your group. You are easy to get along with, and could be self-sacrificing. You can empathize with others well, and may also help them deal with their pain.

G

You're someone who's intellectually active and has a lot of zest and drive for life. You're also someone who knows how to make the best out of every situation and learn from them. You could be systematic, but also often just think on your feet—especially when the situation calls for it, making you one of the most flexible people around.

H

This means that you are quite the visionary. However, the more you make money, the earlier you lose it, too, because you don't often keep track of your finances, which means you'd have to be creative and learn how to get yourself out of various situations, and you have to stop doubting yourself, too.

I

This is a sign that you are compassionate, creative, artsy, and is someone who has a great eye for fashion. You have to learn how to focus, and have the guts to make your dreams come to life—that's how you will find success in life!

J

J stands for justice. You're someone who always tries to find the balance in everything, and is someone who stands for fairness. You are a great friend and you are someone who always tries to make others feel comfortable. You are also a great motivator.

K

This means you are artsy and that you're all about enlightenment. You're someone who can make his own decisions and could easily be motivated, but you have to be mindful of your indecisions and anxiety, too.

L

You're someone who would much rather think than speak or walk easily. You could be quite a workaholic, and you're also someone who doesn't need to sleep much just to feel alert and ready.

M

You're someone who is creative and is not afraid to think out of the box, and be your own person. More often than not, you are a homebody, but could also enjoy careers that are related to finance or business, and the like.

N

You're also someone who is not afraid to think out of the box, and you're probably addicted to blogging or journaling—anything that'll help you save certain memories and make sense of your life. You feel like these can save you from life's entanglements!

O

The O in your name stands for your moral high ground, and the way you see and take life for what you think it is. This also stands for your will, as well as your spiritual beliefs, and also shows that you may have the tendency to be jealous, and to be a fan of routine—and not changing things for a time.

P

P means you are quite knowledgeable and intellectual. While you may seem distant at first, and that you may seem impatient, you're also someone who walks with a lot of sense in his head. Be generous with your time, and learn to let go, as well.

Q

You're a natural money magnet but you have to make sure that you have a stable source of income to help you with your finances. You're quite persuasive and are also a natural leader. You are tough, and you don't easily fall into the traps of desperation.

R

You have a strong need to go outside and see the world around you. You have amazing work ethic and you also know how to provide some sense of balance for your life!

S

You're a devoted, warm, and charming person who also cares quite deeply. Sometimes, you tend to be overly dramatic in life, and you have many ups and downs—while trying to consider every decision, too.

T

You're someone who's quite adventurous and likes to live life in the fast lane. You're also someone who's keen on taking on exciting projects and could also be aggressive when it comes to your relationships—so make sure to provide balance for that.

U

You're someone who believes that "give and take" should be the main philosophy in life. Learn to think on your feet and react to the various changes that life could bring. Be creative and you'll be quite glamorous and easily praised in life, too.

V

You're someone who has great intuition, or a modern seer, for the most part. You're active—whether physically or mentally, and when you're with interesting people, you'd see your charm and charisma growing!

W

You have awesome peace of mind, and has likely found your purpose in life—or is getting there. You like excellent, stimulating conversation—and you often try not to put things off, too!

X

You are a sensual and creative person who easily remembers various kinds of information, which could be quite unsettling, too. You might also be moody, and is the type who hates long conversations.

Y

You're the type who likes to break rules and is all about fun, fun, fun. You might also be reserved or independent—and would rather just do things on your own.

Z

Finally, Z is all about being upbeat and charismatic. You have high understanding—and common sense, too. You also think on your feet, and are just an over-all wise person.

Conclusion

Thank you again for purchasing this book!

I hope this book was able to help you to understand numerology in various forms, and get to understand yourself better, too!

The next step is to use this book as a guide for your life, especially when you feel confused about certain aspects of it!

Finally, if you enjoyed this book, please take the time to share your thoughts and post a review on Amazon. I want to reach as many people as I can with this book, and more reviews will help me accomplish that. It'd be greatly appreciated!

Thank you and good luck!

Jason Williams

Made in the USA
San Bernardino, CA
13 July 2018